1 MONTH OF
FREE
READING

at
www.ForgottenBooks.com

By purchasing this book you are eligible for one month membership to ForgottenBooks.com, giving you unlimited access to our entire collection of over 1,000,000 titles via our web site and mobile apps.

To claim your free month visit:
www.forgottenbooks.com/free1011637

ISBN 978-0-331-07900-5
PIBN 11011637

THE PLACE OF INDUSTRIAL AND TECH-NICAL TRAINING IN POPULAR EDUCATION

In attempting to speak to you upon the matter of Industrial and Technical Training in Popular Education, I am taking up a subject which is receiving at the present time the thoughtful attention of serious and far-sighted men. In order that the consideration of the question which is possible during the present hour may lead somewhither, I shall confine my consideration of the subject to a discussion rather of industrial training and its part in popular education than of the higher forms of technical training. And this for several reasons: First of all, technical training, as we use the word in America, has come to refer to the training of men and women in the higher applications of science. It seeks to equip the officers of the industrial army. This part of the problem of education has for forty years past received a constantly increasing share of our attention, with the result that the number of technical schools and universities in which the higher technical training is given has grown enormously. And whatever may be the merits or faults of our present education, and however far it may be assumed that its present stage is one of transition, it must at least be admitted that the needs of the higher technical training are receiving more attention than almost any other part of our educational processes. In every State in the Union there exist schools for this training for the higher industrial life,—the life of the engineer, of the chemist, of the manager, of the man who in one way or another is to act as a leader in the industrial army. But, after all, the number of leaders who are needed is limited; and it is worth while asking what is being done in America and what can be done for training the sergeants and corporals and privates of the industrial army, the superintendents and foremen and skilled workmen who man our mines and mills, who build our roads and bridges, who make and transport our manufactured products.

There are in this country at present, approximately, 80,000,000 persons. Of this number, approximately 20 per cent., 16,000,000 in all, are between the ages of fifteen and twenty-four,—are eligible, in other words, to the opportunities of the high school and the college. Of this vast number of eligibles, less than one-third of one per cent. are receiving any formal instruction from the State or from private institutions concerning the sciences and arts which bear directly upon their occupations. It is at least worth asking whether our plan of popular education can be made to minister to this vast host which does not now share in its advantages beyond the elementary school.

In order that I may make myself clear, let me ask a moment's consideration of the wording of my subject and the conception of education which it implies. I am to speak to you concerning the place of industrial training in popular education. This language is assumed to apply to the United States, and that the people who are to be educated are those of this country. It assumes, further, that there is to be a popular education, or an education of the people.

Assuming all this, our inquiry concerns itself with the part in this education of the people which industrial and technical training should have; and I have limited the inquiry by confining the discussion to elementary technical training alone.

The subject assumes, furthermore, that there is a distinction between education and training, and that the latter is a factor in the former. The derivation of the word " education " carries a meaning not always remembered. To be educated is to be drawn out. Education embraces all the processes by which a human soul comes to have contact in larger and larger measure with all other souls. It is the resultant of all the forces by virtue of whose influence a human being finds his place in the world. The education is successful when the individual finds for himself the best place which he is capable of filling.

Human souls have various moduli of elasticity. Some are capable of being drawn out in many directions, and attach themselves by the threads of sympathy and interest to every object that offers. Sometimes these tentacles are very foolish ventures, like the thread which a spider spins from his web to the nearest object and directly across the path of the passers-by, only to be swept away. And, then, there are souls of such curious elasticity that they can be stretched out or educated only in one direction, so that ultimately they become hard, tense cords in the general structure of society, and can only be touched by some vibration which is adapted to their particular stress. However it is done or whether it be in large or in small measure, education is that drawing out process of the human soul by which a man finds his place in the world.

But the difficulty which has beset all serious inquirers is the question what to teach in order to educate. Plato and Aristotle, Milton and Rousseau, Spencer and Bain, all agree as to what education is; but the burning question is " how to educate," how to draw out the soul of a man so that it may find its most efficient contact with the world in which he is to live.

Men have agreed by one process or another that one of the most effective ways of stimulating the powers of youth is to bring them together in a school, and to teach them certain things which are believed to assist in the development of the latent powers of the individual. Now it is so much easier to point out the faults of a system of teaching than to indicate the means for correcting those faults that there has never been agreement among schoolmasters as to the subjects which might be taught in the schools in order to develop the qualities of a student. Men ask to-day as anxiously as did Aristotle in his day: " What, then, is education, and how are we to educate? For men are not agreed as to what the young should learn either with a view to perfect training or to the best life."

Furthermore, into most human lives there is thrust the problem of earning a living. So fierce is human struggle at this age that the earning of a livelihood, if the living is to be a comfortable one, requires the possession on the part of the individual of expertness in some one direction. This education in one or more directions to the point of expertness we call training, and training is admitted to be a part of the proper work of the school.

Now, while in America the schoolmasters have no more been able to agree than their brethren in other parts of the world, at least two general theories may be traced in the formation of our schools and colleges. One is the theory that the growing human being should have an opportunity to develop in many ways, that the elastic soul should be encouraged to throw out as many tentacles as possible, and that the system of studies which presents the greatest number of points of attachment is the best one. This process is usually called that of acquiring a broad and liberal education. A second principle, and one that finds almost equal recognition in the institutions of learning of the present day, is the idea that the student must train to the point of expertness in some one direction.

In order to meet these somewhat divergent requirements, we have provided in our higher institutions of learning courses of study intended to minister on the one side to general culture and on the other to special training ; and we undertake to furnish instruction which shall give the student a broader outlook and a wider sympathy, while at the same time he is guided into the straight and narrow path of professional expertness.

The working out of these two theories during the past generation has resulted in the development of two kinds of institution, one of which affords the student a greater or smaller opportunity for education with little or no training, and another which gives him a more or less effective training with little or no education.

Unfortunately, notwithstanding two thousand years of discussion, no criterion has been invented by the application of which it may be determined if a man be entitled to be called an educated man. It is rather by the absence of certain qualifications than by their possession that this test can be applied. Perhaps it would be generally admitted that no man may be fairly termed an educated man until he can read and write his mother tongue with ease and facility, nor until he has some acquaintance with, and has developed some taste for, the best literature of his own country. Judged by even so modest a standard, it seems probable that a large proportion of the graduates of our colleges and scientific schools of to-day are not educated men. One finds amongst these graduates a large number to whom the colleges have brought education without training, and a large number to whom they brought training without education. The two do not always go together. Charles Sumner was a better trained man than Abraham Lincoln. He was not so well educated.

This problem is a vital one before American colleges to-day,— how to combine education with training, how to make a human soul alive to literature, to art, to science, to nature, to religion, to human kinship, and yet at the same time to point out clearly that narrow path which leads to efficiency and economic success. And yet this ought to be possible. A narrow road may have, after all, the widest horizon, if only it leads over the heights.

All this is in one sense apart from the subject under consideration; but it has this relevancy,— that, so far as our discussion of education in this country has crystallized into practice during the past generation, it recognizes that education of the people should minister, in the higher institutions of learning, both to the expanding of the student's horizon and to his special training as well; that in the age in which we live the university should train as well as educate. If this principle is true for those who enter college, it is true in a still larger sense, then, for those who, while carrying on the struggle for existence, are at the same time striving for a wider outlook and a higher efficiency.

The practical question which actually confronts us is this. There are sixteen million persons in the United States between the ages of fifteen and twenty-four. About four millions of these are in high schools and colleges. For twelve millions the opportunity of the regular day-school has gone by. Can a rational and feasible plan be devised by which this large majority of the youth of our country may have opportunity to better themselves by further education, and to increase their efficiency by effective training given in schools such as they can find time to attend?

Let me answer this question, not by indicating an ideal solution, but by briefly describing the way in which the question has been answered in another city, in another land. Fifteen years ago the city of Berlin undertook the solution of this same question. The consideration of the problem was placed in the hands of earnest and thoughtful men. The result of their labors has led to the establishment of a system of secondary technical schools, whose character and function I shall endeavor briefly to describe.

In examining the plans for industrial education in Berlin, one needs to remember that the system of regular day-schools in all German cities includes not only the *Gymnasium* which leads to the university, and the *Realschule* which leads to the higher technical school,— corresponding approximately to our high schools and manual training schools,— but it includes as well a system of secondary schools intended for those who are to follow a particular trade or craft. Each of these secondary technical schools is usually adapted to the branch of technical education needed in the particular district in which it is situated. Where yarns are spun, a spinning school; in the midst of iron works, a school of elementary metallurgy. The instruction, while elementary, is thorough on both the practical and theoretical side; and all the questions involving the success and progress of the special industry are investigated and explained. These schools are neither high-grade engineering schools, like the Institute of Technology, nor are they simple trade schools, like the New York Trade School. Germany has her great technical schools for the higher engineering, and she has trade schools as well, although these latter seldom confine themselves to simple instruction in the trades they represent; but she aims also in these secondary technical schools to meet the wants of those who are to go into commerce or into a trade, to present the opportunity for education, while giving at the same time such minute training as may minister most directly to the calling in life which the pupil is to follow. All these are schools conducted in the ordinary school-houses and in the usual school hours.

But the city of Berlin does not stop here. With characteristic German thoroughness, a system of commercial and industrial education has been planned for those who, while earning a livelihood, are ambitious for further improvement. The system in use is so fully and rationally developed that it deserves a more extended description than I can give here.

These schools are free except in a few cases where small fees are charged, and are held in the evenings and on Sundays from 9 to 12. They may be divided into two classes: (1) continuation schools (*Fortbildungsschulen*), (2) monotechnic, or trade, schools (*Fachschulen*). It would not be fair to call the first class non-trade schools, as they all have a directly practical aim in reference to the student's occupation, either in commercial life or in the trades. The most obvious distinction between these and the second class, or trade schools, is seen in the teaching of German, English, and French in the former, and their omission in the latter. Technical detail is also carried out very much further in the latter. Drawing is almost universally taught, except in a small number of commercial schools. The importance assigned to this subject is characteristic of the German system at large.

It is a general condition for entering both classes of schools that the pupil shall have completed the common school course (the *Volksschule*), which is supposed to be finished at fourteen, the last year of obligatory attendance.

In certain of the special trade schools, as will be mentioned later, it is required that they shall be actual workmen, apprentices, members of a trade, or in training for the counting house.

The first class of schools mentioned (the *Fortbildungs-schulen*, or city continuation schools) are conducted in four groups. One group is devoted to the evening commercial schools. These are intended for persons in practical occupations who are desirous of re-enforcing their acquirements. The subjects taught are German, French, English, mercantile arithmetic, book-keeping, drawing, mathematics, physics, stenography, and typewriting. Four such schools are maintained, each forming an annex to some high-grade institution (either a *Realschule* or a *Gymnasium*) by whose director it is governed. The second group of continuation schools maintained by the city of Berlin is intended to offer to those in a practical calling such advanced studies as may " aid in their calling and strengthen their morals." These schools aim also to make good deficiencies in elementary training. There are twelve such schools for boys supported by the city, and one by the Artisans' Union, attended by some 10,000 pupils. They are all adjuncts of the common schools, using certain rooms in the school buildings, governed by the same principals, and paying their proportionate cost of the school material which is used. Thirteen schools of corresponding character are maintained for girls, attended by nearly 6,000 pupils. Nine of these are supported by the city and four by private effort. The purpose of the girls' school is stated somewhat differently : " to improve their general education, to supply mental stimulus, for fixing serious views of life ; to cherish the inclination and the skill for suitable woman's work." Exclusive attention to technical subjects must be avoided. Both girls and boys are taught German, French, English, arithmetic, drawing (very fully), book-keeping, stenography and typewriting, and to some extent history, geography, and commerce. The boys have certain additional advantages in mathematics, elementary chemistry and physics, and law, together with special advantages in the drawing courses for the trades of lithographer, engraver, decorator, upholsterer, etc. The girls learn needlework, embroidery, machine-work, millinery, and commercial correspondence. Singing and gymnastics are taught in nearly all the schools.

A third group of continuation schools, attended by some 2,500 pupils, is that of mercantile schools. The fourth class of continuation schools is devoted to the teaching of the blind and deaf.

In all there are in the thirty-seven schools of this class over 18,000 pupils, of whom 3,000 are in mercantile schools, the rest in schools looking mainly to the individual development of young artisans in directions favorable to their professional improvement.

The second division of evening schools ministers directly to the special trades, being, in fact, monotechnic schools. The universal aim in these schools is to make up for the loss of formative power (*Bildendekraft*) in shops, due to changed customs and wages, and especially to progressive subdivision of labor. The schools are so varied in character that only the briefest mention can be made of them. Amongst those supported by the city are the city textile school (which is used for one set of pupils during the day and another at night), intended for merchants, journeymen, apprentices, and embroiderers; two artisan schools, supported by the city with some help from the

State, with courses in cabinet-making, painting, modelling, and art-work in metal; the school of architecture, having for its purpose the training of workmen and master-builders; the city tradeshall, a school for those engaged in the trades of locksmith, instrument maker, machine builder, electro-mechanician, and allied branches; the school of joinery, intended to give thorough training to joiners and turners in drawing, modelling, wood-carving, joining, chemical treatment of wood, etc.; and, finally, some twenty-one special trade schools, whose support comes from various sources, but chiefly from the city. The State adds a small quota, and two are supported by the guilds themselves.

The object of these schools is to supply instruction in the trades which cannot be given in the shops. The persons for whom they are intended are primarily apprentices and journeymen. In many trades the apprentices are required to attend. The schools minister to a wide diversity of trades' workers, such as masons, carpenters, shoe-makers, painters, barbers, saddlers and harness-makers, decorators, smiths of all kinds, glaziers, wheelwrights, book-binders, basket-makers, gardeners, printers, tailors, confectioners, photographers, braziers, and coopers. The variety of interests and occupations represented in these schools is most striking, and the dissimilarity in their constitution and government indicates that much has been left to individual initiative. The attendance in these schools is something over 10,000.

A noticeable feature of the whole system is the friendly relation existing between the workmen's guilds and the city schools. The officers of the guilds take a helpful part in the government of the schools, and it is in large measure due to their influence that so many apprentices attend them. In all some 27,000 pupils attend these evening schools in Berlin, either for the purpose of general culture or for helpful training in their own callings; and of this total about 17,000 are apprentices.

So complete is the provision here made for the encouragement of the ambitious youth that any apprentice or any workman may find in these schools the opportunity he seeks, whether it lie in the direction of wider education or in the desire to improve himself in the technique of his trade.

Let us examine for a moment the opportunities open to a youth of Boston similarly circumstanced. Suppose a boy or a girl, a man or a woman, to have completed the grammar school course, and to have begun the earning of a living in some commercial or industrial calling in Boston, as clerk, apprentice, or journeyman : what opportunities are open to such an one for further education and for further training?

The two agencies which the city provides for the education of young wage-earners are represented by the evening high school and the free evening drawing schools, the two taken together constituting a very near approximation to the first group of Berlin continuation schools. In the evening high school a student is offered instruction in arithmetic, algebra (a two years' course), geometry, English (a three years' course), French, German, Latin, chemistry, and physics, book-keeping, stenography and typewriting; and, in the drawing schools, free-hand and mechanical drawing, clay modelling, and the principles of design, composition, and color. Between three and four thousand pupils attend the classes of these evening schools. They serve the same class of pupils as that attending the first and second groups of Berlin continuation schools just

described, and in the main they represent a general simi-
larity of subjects taught. The chief difference between the
two lies partly in the conception of what ought to be taught
and partly in the manner of teaching.

In the Berlin school the German language and literature
are relied upon as the surest and most fruitful source of
culture. It is helped out by elementary mathematics and
physics, taught, however, rather as an aid to the solution of
practical problems in every-day life. In our Boston school
the student is offered more mathematics, more chemistry
and physics, and Latin in addition. Both schools aim to
strengthen the intellectual grasp, while at the same time
aiming to help toward good morals. The one under-
takes to do this by devoting the larger number of hours
to subjects which have a direct bearing in practical life, the
other by devoting the larger number of hours to subjects
which are in the nature of culture studies.

When one seeks, however, in the public evening schools
of Boston any which correspond to those of the second
division of Berlin evening schools, he seeks in vain: they
do not exist. There are no city schools in Boston corresponding to the monotechnic schools of Berlin. Our system of public instruction does not undertake to furnish to
the apprentice or to the clerk or to the journeyman, by
formal instruction, the opportunity for improvement in his
own craft. The ambitious youth in Boston who seeks such
improvement finds open to him the following opportunities
for such training : —

If he be an apprentice, he may avail himself of such
opportunities as the apprentice system offers for improvement in his trade. But it is becoming more and more dif-
ficult for the apprentice to obtain from this relationship the
training which came from it a generation ago. Not only is

the association between master and apprentice no longer what it once was, but the changed functions of modern machinery make smaller the opportunities for getting what the Germans call formative power.

Outside of his employer's office the young workman may turn to one of the following avenues of improvement: In the schools of the Young Men's Christian Association and the Young Men's Christian Union he may obtain certain training bearing upon the work of a trade or a craft. The instruction given by both of these institutions in drawing, modelling, and kindred subjects, is most creditable to those who have charge of these noble organizations. The facilities which their evening schools afford have helped many a man struggling to get a better foothold in his trade or in his craft.

The opportunities which Boston offers to acquire scientific knowledge of a particular trade are limited, and such facilities as exist are maintained by private means. Instruction in practical plumbing and printing may be had by a limited number at the North End Union on payment of a fee of $10 a term. No one under seventeen is admitted, and only those who are already in these trades are taken. Somewhat similar instruction is offered at the South End Union. At the trade school of the Massachusetts Charitable Mechanics' Association, instruction is given to a limited number in three trades,— bricklaying, carpentering, and plumbing. At the North Bennet Street Industrial School, instruction is given in leather-work, printing, clay modelling, basket-work, dressmaking and millinery, cooking and domestic science. Instruction in some of these branches is given at the Wells Memorial Institute. Lessons in cooking and in sanitary housekeeping are offered in the evening by the Women's Educational and Industrial

Union. These schools, maintained by the efforts of private citizens, represent the opportunities for formal instruction in the arts and crafts for working men and women.

Other efforts for such instruction have been made in cities very near Boston, such as the Textile School at Lowell, which is filling so fine a place in the training of men for industrial work ; but these, after all, belong rather to the State than to the city. When all is said, the opportunities open to the young artisan of Boston for self-improvement are meagre compared with those which lie within the reach of the artisan of Berlin.

Somehow, the German plan of using a technical equipment,— for instance, that of a manual training school,— to its full capacity, by instructing one class of pupils in the day and another in the evening, is not one which has as yet commended itself to our American teachers ; and it must be admitted that the teaching of the use of hand-tools in this country, while it undoubtedly offers a valuable addition to the school curriculum, makes this contribution on the academic side. Instruction in manual training forms in this country practically a culture study : it contributes almost nothing to the betterment of those in trades. Granting much that has been claimed for manual training, it seems nevertheless true that, in this country at least, it has done almost nothing to bridge over the difficulties which lie between the untrained apprentice and the skilled artisan. This has been due in some measure, it seems to me, to the great fear which its advocates have had lest it minister to utilitarian ends, and to their intense desire to have it, first of all, rank in dignity with older studies. Their attitude reminds one, in some measure, of the toast offered by a Senior Wrangler, when he said, " Here's to pure mathematics, and may it never be of any use to anybody!"

But the ambitious young man or woman in Boston who is earning a living, and who is willing to struggle for the increased power and pleasure which come from technical knowledge of one's own calling, has not exhausted his opportunities in the night schools maintained by the city and by private thoughtfulness. There has grown up during the last ten years another agency which is within reach of the man who has to make a living, if he can afford it; and this is found in correspondence instruction, given by correspondence schools.

Few college men, I am inclined to believe, are aware of the amount of instruction now being given by these agencies, notwithstanding the fact that two of our universities have, in part at least, committed themselves to a plan for giving instruction in this manner. The number enrolled in correspondence schools at the present time exceeds considerably the total enrolment of all the colleges and technical schools of the United States. While many of those enrolled are studying commercial or English branches, the large majority are endeavoring to obtain in this way technical instruction of an elementary sort. These schools now offer to decorators, to draughtsmen, and to designers instruction in the arts which bear upon their work; to machinists, pattern-makers, foundrymen, blacksmiths, plumbers, sheet-metal workers, miners, carpenters, etc., instruction in their trades; to stationary engineers, locomotive engineers, trainmen, dynamo tenders, linemen, and motormen, instruction in the care and operation of machinery, as well as technical instruction to those who desire to become civil engineers, mechanical engineers, architects, and chemists.

It is no part of my purpose to discuss here the quality of the work accomplished by these correspondence schools or to deal with the question of correspondence instruction; but the enormous proportions to which this enrolment has grown is indicative of two very significant facts. The first is this: In all industries the demand is becoming urgent for men and women who have had sufficient training in applied science to grasp the plans of the engineer above them, and who have the practical knowledge to carry them into execution. The second fact to which I refer is the spectacle itself, of this large number of men and women in the correspondence schools, paying out money earned in many cases with difficulty, and saved only after self-denial, in order to acquire the scientific knowledge necessary to understand the tools with which they are working, and to make the most of these tools. The growth of correspondence schools, whose students are drawn almost wholly from those who are denied a college training, is the most striking evidence which could be presented, not only of the need which such men feel for additional training, but of their determination to obtain it.

It is not necessary to give the complete enrolment of the army of students in the correspondence schools to indicate something of the desire for instruction. In Massachusetts itself more men and women are seeking technical training in correspondence schools than in all other technical schools, public and private, combined. There is to me a touch of pathos in the thought that the efforts of American men and women for a better training have become the foundation of a profitable business.

This completes the enumeration of the avenues open to the wage-earner of Boston who, leaving school at the end of the grammar school period, seeks later on to better himself by a wider education and a more effective training. For the one, he may go to the city evening schools; for the other, he may try apprenticeship, the schools maintained by private enterprise, or the correspondence school maintained by its own enterprise.

When we compare with these the opportunities offered to the youth who begins his industrial or commercial career in Berlin, the contrast is most striking; and the significant feature of the contrast is the fact that the one city presents a system of public education founded upon no effort to study the conditions which are to be met and to meet them, while in the other there is presented a plan which is at least consistent, which rests upon an intelligent study of the whole question of the education of the people, and which aims to meet in a rational way the varying wants of all classes.

I have thought it worth while to spend so much of this hour in a comparison of educational opportunities in two specially chosen cities, not for the purpose of suggesting that we in Boston should blindly follow what has been done in Berlin, but rather for other reasons which I will endeavor to state briefly.

First of all, I desired that the discussion of this hour should not be wasted, and that it should lead somewhither. It has, for this reason, seemed to me wiser to point to a definite effort to meet the conditions of modern life by education and training than to talk of abstractions. It is never a waste of time to call attention to the fact that all truth and all wisdom are not confined to one nation or to one sect or to one party. The nations of Europe have been trying social experiments longer than we. I believe we may safely learn something from their experience if we approach the problem in the right spirit.

The Berlin experiments of the last fifteen years are especially worth our study, because those who have there had the matter in hand have endeavored to struggle, not with a partial solution of the problem of education and training, but with the problem as a whole; and, in doing this, they have recognized fully the two ideas which have been most dominant in American educational processes for the past generation, namely: that the teaching of the schools must aim, not only to educate, but to train; and the converse, that it is not enough simply to train in the school, but that the school should educate as well. Not only have they recognized these two needs, but, keeping both in mind, they have not hesitated to grapple with the fact that different groups of students enter the preparatory schools with widely varying purposes in view, and that these purposes must be kept in mind in the education of these boys and girls. They have taken the view that, if the truths and processes of modern science and of art were helpful to the leaders in the industrial world, they could be no less helpful, if taught in the right way, to those in the ranks. Admitting all these facts, they have gone on to offer to the youth of their city a system of schools planned in a consistent and intelligent way to meet, not the wants of a single class or of a single trade, not a hard-and-fast system, but a system at once comprehensive, elastic, and representative of the whole people. And whether the solution which Berlin has reached be a wise one or not, whether it accomplishes the entire end for which it is aimed or not, it is at least worthy of our study as being an intelligent, a comprehensive, and a systematic effort to do that which in Boston we are doing in a desultory and a partial way.

The study of the Berlin system of industrial technical

schools conducted for wage-earners has for us another point of still greater significance, which is found in the attitude of organized labor toward these schools. The Berlin industrial schools are being conducted with the co-operation and with the help of the artisans themselves, and of the trades-unions into which they are organized. There has been an impression that in this country the trades-unions are hostile to industrial schools. I do not know how much truth there is in such an assertion. Organized labor in America has sometimes been unfortunate in its leaders, and has been thereby betrayed into some foolish and short-sighted actions. For myself, I have faith in the sincerity and in the ultimate fairness of the real American workman, whether born on this side of the Atlantic or the other. I believe that he will not be slow to see that industrial schools are to mean to him the quickest road to power and to independence which organized society has yet offered to him. But, whether this be true or not, it is certainly true that the first step to success in such an undertaking is the co-operation and interest of workingmen themselves, and of the organizations through which they express themselves. Men are never reformed from without or against their wills. By the same token they do not permit themselves to be educated from without or against their wills, and the first and wisest step in any system of industrial education is to enlist the interest and the confidence of those who are to be educated.

The reasons put forward by the advocates of a system of industrial schools for this country are usually based upon utilitarian considerations. They point to the example of Germany, and urge that her industrial success has been due in large measure to her system of education, and that success rests not only upon the officers of her industrial army drawn from the high-grade technical schools, but upon the rank and file trained in the industrial schools as well. Without similar training, they say, we are likely to fall behind in the race for industrial supremacy. I believe there is much truth in these claims, and that they alone form a sufficient reason for a careful consideration of elementary technical training as a part of our system of popular education. There are other reasons, however, that to my mind appeal more strongly than any consideration of dollars and cents, even when that glittering prize "industrial world-supremacy" is held out as the trophy of success.

One reason, and a primary one, for the establishment of schools for commercial and industrial training as a part of a system of popular education, is the fact that a system of popular education should in reality be what it calls itself, a system of education for the people and for the whole people. As our schools are at present maintained, the people, as a whole, share in them only up to a certain point; and, while it is true that the opportunity to continue in the high schools is open to every citizen, it is in fact closed by stress of circumstances over which pupils themselves have but little control. The average schooling for the entire nation is at present eight hundred and sixty days for each person. This would give four years and three-tenths, allowing two hundred days to each school year, enough to take a pupil through the primary schools of a city. Even Massachusetts, with all its schools, public and private, does not give enough schooling to amount to seven years apiece for its inhabitants. Some States of the Union give, on the average, only a little more than two years. It is worth noting in this direction that Massachusetts, with nearly twice the average schooling per individual, produces twice the amount of wealth per individual as compared with the nation's average.

I have always been at some loss to account for the fact that 80 per cent. of all children are withdrawn from school upon the completion of the preparatory school course, even in well-to-do communities. It is due not wholly to poverty and to the need for the services of the boy or girl, but also to the feeling of the parents that the schooling to be acquired by a longer stay is of no practical benefit in the trade or in the commercial career which the pupil is to attempt. Many of the pupils withdrawn realize in a very short time the need of a better education and a higher training; and, to my thinking, it is most desirable that some door easily accessible be left open to that great majority of our youth outside the schools, by which they may find the education which may minister to breadth of view and the training which may help toward efficiency. Such an opportunity means not only a great increase in skill and in power for a large part of our population, but it means as well an enormous influence which shall work for a higher form of manhood and of womanhood.

Further, the introduction of industrial and commercial preparatory schools into our educational scheme will serve, not only as a partial corrective to certain tendencies which now tempt boys and girls away from the lines in which they might be most useful, but by putting forward the opportunities for a better form of commercial and industrial training will help to maintain the dignity of labor itself.

The following abstract from the report of a well-known officer of the Navy engaged in recruiting apprentices for the Navy is suggestive of certain tendencies in our education in New England which need to be taken into account in any study of a present and possible system of public instruction : —

" I enlisted boys from all parts of the country, and necessarily saw the conditions surrounding the poorer classes in many cities. After one trip to Boston, where I enlisted several hundred boys, I was satisfied that education, or rather over-education, was doing great harm in New England. Book schools were not doing what industrial schools would have accomplished. Each morning, when I went to my office at the Navy Yard Gate, I found a long line of fairly well-dressed boys with very shabbily dressed parents. In every case the boy had spent his life in school, winding up in many cases in the high school, and after that finding nothing to do. The parents were striving hard and stinting themselves that the boys might appear well, while the lads were growing up more and more ashamed of themselves and of their surroundings, and of their honest fathers and mothers. To save them from pool-rooms and worse, they begged me to take them as apprentices in the Navy, and let them begin anew their education."

Inasmuch as the large majority of all who enter the common schools have eventually to earn their bread by some form of labor, whether it be on the farm or in commerce or in the arts and crafts, it is worth while to have such recognition of this fact in at least some of the schools as will make a boy or girl proud to prepare himself or herself for such a life. We have grown too much accustomed in our schools and in our colleges to hold out the extraordinary rewards of college education or of technical training as a reason for education and for training. The " room at the top" motto has been overworked. To urge upon young men the advantages of college education and of college training, because this engineer or that chemist has achieved extraordinary financial or popular success, is in some ways similar to inviting them to invest in a lottery. Schools and colleges exist not for the preparation of the few great successes, but because we believe that the education for which they stand is a preparation for a wiser, more useful and more contented life. It is equally desirable that the State should say to a still larger class of citizens that in the pursuits of commerce and industry they may find a life which satisfies the intellectual and artistic and moral aspirations of men, to commend to them the life of industrial and commercial effort for its own sake.

And, finally, such schools seem to me most desirable in a democratic government as a means of holding together by a common thread of interest the whole body of citizens. It will be a bad day for our institutions when those who work with their hands come to feel that they have any smaller interest in our common schools than has any other class of citizens. Men have seen, during the last generation, the conserving influence in society weakened at many points. Two generations ago master and apprentice met on a common plane at the meeting-house. To-day it is a far cry from the man who sits in a pew to the man who tends the dynamo supplying the light by which the minister reads his sermon. In the problems that face us in the future it is most necessary that distinctions of class be not further accentuated. There is no surer way to promote this desired solidarity than by a system of education in which those who direct the education are kept in touch with the great body of citizens. There is no common thread of interest running through the whole fabric of our political life better calculated to exert a unifying touch upon all classes of citizens than that which has to do with public education. For this reason, if for no other, it is vital that education in a republic minister to the whole people, and that it consider in its ministry the needs of those whom it is to serve.

And now, one naturally asks, what is the practical change

which should be made in order to make our public school system minister to the wants of all the people? What schools can be added to those already maintained which shall serve the double purpose of education and training? How should they be organized, by whom controlled, and how maintained, in order to serve in the widest sense the whole people?

Such an inquiry is a perfectly fair one. It is the one toward which our whole discussion has led us. Unless it can be answered in a practical way, such discussions have no purpose. I shall endeavor to reply to it as directly as it seems possible to do.

First of all, it seems to me that, if one suddenly found in his hands the arbitrary power to make changes in our system of popular instruction, he would neither add to it new features nor take from it old ones, for the present; that, looking back over the evolution of our present schemes of education (we can scarcely call them systems), he would recognize that these educational processes are still in a transition stage. Forty years ago, and following the Civil War, a mighty desire for education came upon us. For a time we believed that all education was good, and the more of it, the better. Every institution in the land strained to the utmost to teach every subject,— a theory which found its perfect fruit in the idea that every institution must teach every subject to every student. All the doctors in education have been allopaths.

After a while we discovered that this was all wrong, and a new set of doctors came in who believed in educational specifics. The number of special studies and methods of training which have been put forward in the last twenty years, warranted to be infallible educators for man and beast, would almost equal the number of patent medicines.

The experience of our schools is painfully like that of a gentle Oriental nation which undertook to found a university. Those who had in their hands the appointment of professors had a theory that any American or any Englishman could teach any subject. Accordingly, a faculty was selected at the nearest seaport from amongst the butchers and sailors. The results were interesting, but hardly satisfactory. There were periods when the entire faculty was disabled for days as the result of prolonged investigation of the physical qualities of *spiritus frumenti*. Gradually the officials in charge of the university arrived at the generalization that not all foreigners could teach. The sailors were accordingly sent about their business, and a faculty selected who were all missionaries. The result was an enormous improvement, but still not all that was hoped for. Modern dynamos and problems in recent chemical processes were troublesome to men educated in Latin and Greek and theology. After five years more, that pleasing Oriental government made another generalization, one worth acquiring even at the price paid ; and it was this,— that not only all foreigners could not teach all subjects, but that, if a given subject was to be effectively taught, a teacher must be secured who had fitted himself to teach that particular subject.

It seems to me that we have arrived at a point in our experiments in popular education when certain generalizations are possible. Some of them would seem to be the following : —

One school cannot teach every subject, still less can it teach every subject to every student.

There is such a thing as too much teaching, and there is such a thing as teaching too much.

There are no specifics in education. No subject and no

special method of presenting that subject, and no particular process of training, can be warranted to make an educated man out of an uneducated boy or a trained man out of an untrained boy.

On the other hand, the outcome of our universal human experience goes to show that no man may any longer call any branch of human knowledge common or unclean, or the teaching of it without value to some soul, if one only knew when and how and to whom to teach it.

And, having accepted these generalizations, it would seem to follow that the things to be taught a given class of students will depend, to a degree at least, upon the environment and the life purpose of the students. And so, after all, one comes back to the thought that, since the life in school or in college is not an isolated one, but a part of the life of the world, the teaching in them should have relation to the life in the world. But the question, What teaching shall minister to a particular class of lives? is, after all, a question of individual human judgment. And, having come thus far, I am inclined to feel that I would follow the example of my Oriental friends and ask the assistance of those whose judgment seems, on the whole, the best worth following. And from this standpoint the question of adding to our present public school system that which shall minister to industrial training becomes simply a part of the larger and more important question, What ought that system to be, and how ought it to be conducted?

In a very real sense we are struggling with this question in every American city to-day. We struggle with it perennially in Boston whenever we undertake to elect a school committee. No one who has at heart the true interest of the city can fail to understand the need for the election of capable and honest men to the body which controls and which conducts our schools. And yet, after all, this is only at best the first step in the problem. The school committee itself is a part of a system which was effective a hundred years ago, but long since obsolete. At some time or other, and in some way or other, we shall need to undertake the serious consideration of what the school shall endeavor to do in the education and in the training of the whole people ; and for the solution of this question we shall need to summon to our aid not only those who are intellectually able and intellectually sincere, but those who represent, as well, the convictions and the aspirations of our entire citizenship.

By some such intelligent effort as this, and only in some such way, shall we finally come to a solution of what ought to be taught in a system of popular education ; and only by such means shall we arrive at a solution which is consistent, rational, and democratic, and which shall embody in it with a fair perspective that which aims toward a wider culture of the soul and that which aims toward economic efficiency. In any system so devised by thoughtful and representative men, industrial and technical schools, adapted to the needs of those they are to serve, will assuredly find a place.

HENRY S. PRITCHETT.